This book is dedicated to the man that broke my heart.. Thank you.

TABLE OF CONTENTS

Disclamer

TABLE OF CONTENTS

01
THE RAIN

*"IN THE DEPTHS OF WINTER, I FINALLY LEARNED THAT WITHIN ME
THERE LAY AN INVINCIBLE SUMMER."
- ALBERT CAMUS*

Before we begin...

Before you read my story...

Before you start this journey...

I need you to know that you are valuable, you are worthy of love, and there are people in this world that need you.

You will find the light again. And by the end of this journey,

I hope that you will realize that you are the light.

Heartbreak, not one person on this Earth, is immune to it. It is an unavoidable part of the human experience. At times, heartbreak can bring real physical pain. Like that awful pit in the bottom of your stomach, or those pains in your chest that seemingly come out of nowhere. But what probably hurts the most is the hole your ex leaves behind, the emptiness in your life. The space they used to fill in your day and your life is gone. All you have left are the memories. Without your ex, life seems less enjoyable. Your thoughts are all over the place, and you just want to feel normal again, happy, at least I did.

What I remember most about the day it happened was the rain. It was early spring in Washington,

> STRENGTH GROWS IN THE MOMENTS WHEN YOU THINK YOU CAN'T GO ON, BUT YOU KEEP GOING ANYWAY.
> ~UNKNOWN

D.C., and rainy days are a natural occurrence, but this rain, this rain was so different. If I were the type of person to look for signs, it surely would have been in the clouds forming outside my bedroom window that Monday morning.

My boyfriend and I had an intense argument the night before, and I woke up the next morning thinking things would be icy between us. He called me on his way to work as I lay in bed. We exchanged our usual morning pleasantries, and I felt good. We'd argued before. I figured we would talk through our issues and come to an understanding. But as our conversation continued, it became clear that he was much more affected by our argument than I had realized. He began to explain how he felt we weren't working as a couple, how we weren't compatible, and how his vision for the future didn't include an "us." "We're just on different paths in life," he said, "Our goals don't align." He felt that we each navigated the world so differently, and had opposing views on so many different things. He didn't think we were a good match. In his eyes, we weren't equally yoked. I knew from the tone of his voice and the tempo of his words that this conversation was hard for him. I could also tell that this was something he had given a lot of thought to, and it wasn't a decision born from just one argument. He was done. The relationship was over.

I was stunned. The entire conversation caught me entirely off guard. We had recently returned from a 10-day vacation to Thailand. We had what I thought was the time of our lives; I even described our trip to friends and family as "the trip of a lifetime." I just couldn't wrap my mind around his words. I offered a few words of resistance. I told him he was not making the right decision. I reminded him of all the fun we had and the good times we had shared. In the end, my words made no difference. So I listened a bit more. I let go of my ego, and I received what he was saying to me. I then thanked him for his honesty and told him goodbye.

I am a proud woman, and certainly not the type to beg a man to stay with me when he doesn't want to. Pulling up the covers, I curled up into the tightest ball I possibly could. I set my eyes to my bedroom window and shifted my entire focus to that rain...that unending rain

I remember that it rained for days. Not the warm spring rain you look forward to because you know it will yield beautiful flowers. No, this was a relentless, depressing, unwavering rain. A rain that went on for days and days, a rain that I started to believe would never ever end.

For the next few days, I stayed home telling my children, who grew increasingly concerned that

AT SOME POINT I DUCKED OUT. I CAUGHT AN UBER AND CRIED THE ENTIRE WAY HOME.

their mother was in bed for days in the fetal position and coworkers that I had a nasty stomach virus. Texts and calls from friends went unanswered. I was heartbroken. My appetite was nonexistent, and my eyes were dry and swollen from crying. I had no desire to leave from the refuge that was my bed. I cried almost nonstop and slept maybe 2-3 hours a night. Sometimes I didn't feel like I had the strength to move. I would lay in bed, still in disbelief. At night I would pray to God to save me from this pain. It was the worst heartache I have ever felt. But somewhere, deep down, a part of me remained hopeful. As I lay there in bed, I was hoping, waiting for a text or a call from him saying he had changed his mind, that he made a terrible mistake and was missing me just as much as I was missing him.

No such call or text came.

By Thursday, I mustered the strength to go to work. I even dressed up as I had a birthday dinner to attend that evening, and one of my best friends and her boyfriend were coming into town. It was hard; work was hard, and a couple's dinner, where a newly single me had to answer questions about where he was and why we had suddenly broken up, was unquestionably hard. "But you looked so happy, what happened?" they asked. "Was there someone else?"

Chapter 1 | The Rain

I didn't know. I wish I had those answers to give. It is difficult to answer questions that you yourself are desperately seeking the answers to. My friends were very understanding and listened as I told them my version of events. The evening went on, and dinner was followed by drinks and dancing at a beautiful lounge. I normally love lounges and spending time with my friends, so I continued to smile through my sadness, but it was tough. Eventually, it became apparent to everyone that I wasn't having any fun. I loved that my friends were there with their significant others, sharing inside jokes and knowing glances, but it served as a reminder that I wouldn't have that with him anymore.

At some point, I ducked out, caught an Uber, and cried the entire ride home.

The pain was agonizing. I could not think. I could not eat. I could not sleep. Sometimes I felt like I couldn't breathe. It was like the bottom had dropped out of my life. Friday came, and I felt relieved knowing I only had to make it through the workday, and then I could spend the evening and the next two days curled up in bed, crying my eyes out. And that is exactly what I did.

It was our second breakup. The first breakup happened after we had dated for about six months. I broke up with him for something that, as I look back on it, seems silly. He didn't answer my calls one night. I didn't believe his answer about attending a work function and falling asleep after returning home. Instead of having a conversation with him about how not reaching him made me feel deeply insecure, I ended the relationship. He seemed disappointed but didn't put up much of a fight. This breakup was nothing that a few girls nights out, and a few dates with new suitors couldn't cure.

Oddly enough, this breakup happened in the spring as well, but the sun was shining, and I brushed myself off and went on to have a pretty great spring and an awesome summer. Fall came around, and we bumped into each other at a singles event and struck up a conversation. It was great seeing him again, and we left the singles event together and went to one of our old favorite hookah lounges. Some of our friends joined us just like old times. We became inseparable. We went on dates, spent the holidays together, introduced our children to each other, traveled, and discussed our future wedding and the beautiful marriage that would come with it.

I was all in. This relationship was meant to be I thought, how could it not be?

So now you know the story of my heartbreak.

What is your story?

What was the moment that led you to this book?

Chapter 1| The Rain

Writing/Journal Exercise:

During my breakup, I found journaling was a great way to process my feelings. Through writing, I prioritized my thoughts and processed my emotions even when they seemed overwhelming. This journaling exercise will allow you to process your emotions and get clear about what you are feeling. When we experience complicated feelings, it can be hard to sift through all of the different thoughts about what we're going through. By sitting down and writing in your journal, you take the time to slow your mind down. You are able to think about all of the parts of your current experience.

I'm sure you have replayed the breakup or the end of your relationship in your mind a thousand or so times. You may have even told a friend or two what happened, but now you are going to write it out. You are going to tell your story, in your own words, every gory detail of it. I want you to get deep into the weeds with the who, what and why. You will even write the parts that you tend to omit to paint yourself or your ex in a slightly better light. There is freedom in truth, and it is time for you to be free. In this exercise, you are going to free yourself from the weight of the end of your relationship. This freedom will come through writing out your story and then making peace with it once and for all.

"Those convinced against their will are of the same opinion still." ~ Dale Carnegie

You no longer need to hold on to the story or the pain that it brings. You have the power to free yourself from that pain. And you will. You are going to make peace with the way things ended, even if it was ugly. Even if an ending was the last thing you wanted.

There is no longer a need to replay those last moments in your head over and over. There is no longer a need to think of things you could have said to change their mind. You cannot control other people. What happened has happened, and there was nothing you can do to change it.

This is the journey to healing your broken heart.

Your Story

There is freedom that comes with telling your truth.
Use the space below to get it all out once and for all.
The Good, The Bad, and The Ugly.

Your Story

There is freedom that comes with telling your truth.
Use the space below to get it all out once and for all.
The Good, The Bad, and The Ugly.

Your Story

There is freedom that comes with telling your truth.
Use the space below to get it all out once and for all.
The Good, The Bad, and The Ugly.

Your Story

There is freedom that comes with telling your truth.
Use the space below to get it all out once and for all.
The Good, The Bad, and The Ugly.

THE JOURNEY PROMISE

Welcome to 28 Days Under the Sun - The Ultimate Guide to Healing from Heartbreak. As you finish each chapter, you will make a promise. These promises are yours and yours alone, and they will help you as you move through your breakup. This first Promise is the simplest, but the most important. It is not only a promise but a decision, the decision to heal your broken heart.

I PROMISE TO...

begin the journey to heal my broken heart. I am ready and willing to move forward with my life, leaving any hurt, pain, and trauma from this relationship behind. I commit myself today, to healing and moving beautifully forward to the next great thing in my life.

CHAPTER

NEW REALITY
02

"CLOSURE IS AN ILLUSION, THE WINKING OF THE EYE OF A STORM.
NOTHING IS COMPLETELY RESOLVED IN LIFE, NOTHING IS PERFECT.
THE IMPORTANT THING IS TO KEEP LIVING BECAUSE ONLY BY LIVING
CAN YOU SEE WHAT HAPPENS NEXT." ~ PATTI SMITH

I hate mornings most of all. I wake up and look at my phone and realize you haven't called. There is no good morning text to greet me, and I am quickly reminded that we have broken up. As I ease out of bed to begrudgingly start my day, I remember that you will not call me before work to chat. There will be no call during my morning commute as we prepare for our day. There is no loud talk radio blasting in the background for me to remind you to turn down so I can hear you. There are no complaints from you about how high the daily toll is, even though you know it will be high every day. I miss you so much, and it's hard to face this reality day in and day out. I go back and forth between hoping we can find a way to work things out to despising you and regretting the day we met.

After a breakup, sometimes we are lucky, and reality sets in pretty quickly. This is good because the faster you begin to process the reality of the situation, the faster you can move on to healing your broken heart. Now for some of you (like me) it may take a little longer for the reality of the breakup to set in. I am going to help you with this. You must read these words, take them in, and apply them to your relationship with your ex. These words are not meant to hurt your feelings, but to help you heal.

You and your ex have broken up for a reason, whether you agree with that reason or not.

You cannot force someone to care about you. You cannot force someone to love you.

Sometimes the person you want the most is the person you are better off without. You must stop breaking your own heart by trying to make a relationship work that is not meant to work. You cannot force someone to be loyal or to be the person you need them to be. Some things in life are indeed meant to happen but are ultimately not meant to be. Some people are meant to come into your life, but they are not meant to stay. Do not lose yourself by trying to fix what is meant to stay broken. You can't get the relationship you need from someone who is not ready and willing to give it to you. You may not understand why now, but your future will always bring an understanding about why things didn't work out the way you had planned. Trust and believe in this! Some chapters in life just have to close without closure.

There is a Zen proverb that says, "Let go or be dragged."

I love this proverb because it is very easy to interpret and it gets straight to the point. How long will you hold onto your past and try to force things to work? How long will you sit waiting, hoping that your ex will somehow find their way back to you? How long will you continue to wait for someone to come back who has shown you that they do not value your presence in their life?

Let's say hypothetically, that you are able to beg, or otherwise convince your ex to come back to you or to stay with you. What would that look like? Imagine a person who knows that no matter what they do or say, they know that you will do and allow anything just to keep them in your life. As wonderful as your ex

YOU CAN'T GET THE RELATIONSHIP YOU NEED FROM SOMEONE WHO IS NOT READY AND WILLING TO GIVE IT TO YOU

might be, they may end up taking advantage of that fact. They may begin to resent the fact that you are clinging to them for dear life. You, my friend, deserve so much more. You deserve a love that doesn't need convincing of how great you are. You deserve a love that you don't have to beg for. You deserve a love that wants you just as much as you want it.

It is time to let go.

You must let go of this person who does not want a relationship with you anymore. I know it hurts, and the only thing that can stop the hurt is them. But you must let go, or be dragged. Accept the idea of letting go, and let go with love. Letting go doesn't mean you no longer love them, because you probably always will, but, you've chosen to put yourself and your healing first.

When you let go with love, you free yourself. You cannot convince someone to love you.

Make the conscious decision Today to let this person go.

Make peace with what was. People either love you or they don't. They either accept you, or they don't. They either choose to stay with you no matter what, or they choose to leave. The sooner you understand this, the sooner you will be able to let go of people, places, and situations that no longer need your presence. Making peace with the past happens when you no longer waste time, attention, and energy on things that cannot be changed. You can only learn from your past and take corrective actions in the present. Analyzing, overthinking, and regret are just wastes of your time. None of these things changes anything that has already happened.

Surrender and trust that everything will be okay. Just as light is the absence of darkness, surrender is the absence of trying to control everything.

"Let go of the illusion that it could have been any different." ~ Jeff Foster

Know that no matter how dark things feel, brighter days are sure to come.

Help yourself move forward by embracing the natural flow of your life. Understand that people come and go in our lives, and sometimes we have no choice but to let go of the old and embrace a new reality. Life's challenges offer a gateway through which we can learn and grow and transition into a new era in life.

Change is the only constant in our lives. As much as we may try to hang on to things in life, we must remember that life is always in flux. By refusing to accept this, you resist life itself. Remember that even if you lose everything, you are still you. Nothing that happens can erase who you are. You are always you, no matter what happens.

Experiences may change you, but deep inside, there is still that perfect inner light, the framework of who you truly are. You can't change what has happened, but you can choose to allow this moment to teach you something about yourself, even if it is difficult.

Let it go Exercise:

I want you to take the next 15-20 minutes and mentally let go. Find a quiet space where you can be alone with your thoughts. I want you to think about your old relationship. Remember all the good times you shared. Honor what you had, and begin to appreciate the lessons learned. If you need to journal, feel free to, now is the time. The experiences you shared with your ex are still meaningful, and those moments are still a part of your life's story. After you have finished reminiscing and honoring the space that was your relationship, mentally picture yourself walking away. There is no turning back. Release the hope of reconciliation, and the hope that they will someday return to you. You are walking in a new direction. You are walking away with fond memories and experiences and a smile in your heart. The experiences you had are no less valuable because you two aren't together anymore. These experiences have shaped you and added richness to your life. Picture yourself moving on, deliciously anticipating the next great thing that is coming your way. Mentally move forward toward a big bright, beautiful sun and a life filled with endless possibilities. There is so much more available to you in life, and you will begin to see it once you finally let go.

THE FREEDOM PROMISE

Make a promise to let go of the past. Holding on will not bring your ex back. Accept what has led you to this moment. Be thankful for the experiences you had, and embrace the wonderful possibilities that lie ahead.

I PROMISE TO...

let go completely. I am no longer bound to an old relationship that doesn't exist anymore. I am thankful for what was, and I am ready for what will be. Today I am free.

5 STAGES OF GRIEF DURING A BREAK UP

Grieving the end of a relationship is completely natural. Knowing the stages of grief can help normalize the breakup experience for you. There is no timeline or deadline for getting over your heartbreak, so let go of the pressure to feel better right away. According to David Kessler, there are five stages of grief, and "The five stages of grief – denial, anger, bargaining, depression, and acceptance – are a part of the framework that makes up our learning to live without the one we lost. They are tools to help us frame and identify what we might be feeling, but they are not stops on some linear timeline in grief." (Kessler)

DENIAL

In the beginning, your heart is in charge. Your heart is calling all the shots. As your mind tries to process what is happening, and adjust to the idea of life without the person you love, your heart is in denial. You don't believe that this happened to you. I mean sure, you may have had the actual breakup conversation, or text or email, but you don't actually believe that the relationship is over. You hold out hope for a text or a phone call from your ex that they've made a terrible mistake and cannot imagine life without you. You cling to a small glimmer of hope that this was all a bad dream, and tomorrow things will go back to the way they were.

ANGER

Anger can manifest in many ways. There is anger at your ex: How could they do this to me? Why did you have to hurt me like this? Anger at God or the Universe. Why don't things ever work out for me? Why am I so unlovable? Anger at people or situations associated with the breakup, like a third-party involved with your ex. Anger at other people like friends and family who chose to stay neutral. "Can you believe Mark and Julia still want to be friends with him after what he did to me?" Anger is the stage where we think it's a great idea to tell anyone and everyone what a crazy psycho our ex was. This stage is also when we tend to do mean things, or think it's necessary to send our ex hateful texts because we don't want them thinking they got away with anything.

BARGAINING

Bargaining usually comes along with denial. Bargaining includes looking for any possible way to make the relationship work, whether trying to convince your ex they've made a mistake, threatening them, and even trying to use "magic." Trying to win your ex back by telling them that you will go to therapy, or change, or move, anything to get them to change their mind is all bargaining. Bargaining is not only limited to bargaining with your ex; many people bargain with The Powers That Be, vowing to be a better person if only the ex will come back. You may take a new interest in astrology, tarot cards, or anything that will predict some future reunion during this stage. This stage is also when we might attempt to enlist all friends and family to "talk some sense" into our ex.

DEPRESSION

Depression, like anger, also surfaces in many forms. For example, you feel tired all the time, not wanting to do anything but lay in bed, feeling disconnected from people even when you're with them. Trouble sleeping or sleeping too much, loss of appetite, or overeating. Increase in drug or alcohol use and the worst of all, hopelessness. Hopelessness is relatively common and often debilitating; it is the thing that leads us to believe that nothing will ever feel different or be better than it is right now. Hopelessness makes it feel like you will never move on, and things will never work out for you in the future.

ACCEPTANCE

Finally, this is the stage in which we make peace with the end of the relationship. It doesn't always come on right away. It often happens gradually, and sometimes we have to work to get there. Acceptance doesn't always look and feel the way we want it to. We want to come peacefully, but it usually comes with some lingering sadness. Acceptance means making peace with the end and letting the relationship go. It entails moving forward with your life. Sometimes it feels like this phase will never come, which usually means you're still struggling in one of the earlier stages. (Kessler)

This book is designed to help you move through the healing process. Recognize that you may be going through different phases of the grieving process as you heal. You may find yourself stuck in one stage, and that is okay. Acknowledge where you are in your journey and know that what you feel is normal, and you are not alone. Remember, that this like everything else, will eventually pass.

CHAPTER

FEELINGS

THINKING YOU'RE COMING BACK VERSUS FORGETTING YOU EXIST.
SOME DAYS IT'S LIKE WE NEVER EVEN HAPPENED, SOME DAYS IT
FEELS LIKE IT ALL HAPPENED YESTERDAY...

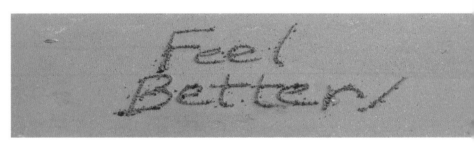

There are breakups, and there is THE breakup. We've all broken up with someone we weren't really vibing with. Perhaps they did something trivial that you could never see yourself willingly dealing with, or maybe they broke up with you for reasons you don't care to know about or don't even care to remember one week later. And then there is THE breakup. The one that feels like a truck hit you...*I spent night after night staring at the ceiling, crying myself to sleep. I would wake up with massive pains in my chest after dreaming of him. I fall asleep in the same bed he used to frequent, and it feels so empty now...This hurt is different. It's a hurt you can't see past, a hurt that's triggered every time you hear your favorite song or any song for that matter. There were songs that I* had heard on the radio a thousand times, and suddenly, now that I was heartbroken, I heard every word, devoured them, and applied them to my now-defunct relationship.

I remember my best friend invited me to do karaoke one night, and I ended up damn near running out of the place because I couldn't stop bawling my eyes out. Every song was somehow a thinly veiled tribute to me and my ex. It was brutal. And even though I was in a room filled with people, I felt so alone in my pain. Well-meaning friends and family would share their advice on a breakup or two that they managed to heal from, but I thought there was no way they could understand the level of pain I was in. We were in love, like madly, deeply in love, and it just ended so abruptly. No, they couldn't

My feelings changed from day to day, and although I thought about my ex all of the time, there were days I felt nothing...but there were also days I felt everything.

possibly understand, this hurt I was feeling was otherworldly. I thought no one could or would ever really comprehend what I was feeling. So I isolated myself.

I went to work every day, numb and sad. Eventually, I decided I would allow myself to cry as much as I needed to. I also decided I would try to binge watch a funny series hoping to laugh to take my mind off my sorrow. So every day after work, I threw on my pj's, climbed into bed, and cried, and from time to time, I laughed. My children were spending a lot of time with their dad, so thankfully, they didn't see their mom's new routine of crying and binge-watching daily. I turned down many invites for nights on the town and fun with friends. People would be there, and I wasn't quite ready for people, especially male people. It was sad. I was sad. A sadness I just couldn't shake.

Two months into the breakup and things were slightly more manageable. At work, I still had to sneak off to the bathroom to cry my eyes out privately, but most days, I was okay. There are other days, though, where it felt like we just broke up yesterday. Sometimes a random memory that I had long forgotten would hit me like a ton of bricks. Like that time, my ex bought a new car online on a whim, and I drove two hours with him to go pick it up. The time we went to see his favorite singer, and he danced in the aisles and sang every song word for word at the top of his lungs. Or when someone mentions a restaurant, and I remember that we ate there and made up silly songs about how great the food was. Those memories seem to come flooding back.

Although I was feeling mildly better, my emotions were all over the place. They changed from one day to the next, from one moment to the next. When things were hard, I felt like I was spinning in circles, going nowhere. Some days were good though, and I kept trying to find those days. I intended to stay positive because, if I let it, the sadness would drown me.

PAIN IS TEMPORARY, LOVE YOURSELF THROUGH IT - LELAH DELIA

Figure out your feelings

As you move through your breakup, your feelings will change. For me, sometimes, my feelings changed almost daily. Although I thought about my ex all the time, there were days that I felt nothing. And then there were days that I felt absolutely everything. When people would ask me how I was doing or feeling, I typically responded with "okay." In reality, I wasn't even sure if I was okay. I needed a way to figure out what I was feeling, and that's when I found the emotion and feeling wheel composed by the Junto Institute (Chadha). This tool made it easier for me to identify how I felt and helped guide me to look deeper at those feelings.

Take a look at the emotion and feeling wheel on the next page. Each wedge represents a core human emotion, like love, joy, anger, or fear. Once you find the core emotion you feel, you can then identify the more specific emotions related to the core emotion. For example, while I felt overall sadness that my relationship ended, when I really looked at what I was feeling, I realized the specific emotion I felt was disappointment.

I was disappointed that we had broken up, disappointed that my ex wasn't who he said he would be for me, disappointed that he didn't keep the promises made and that the outcome of our relationship wasn't the outcome I had hoped for. But mainly, I was disappointed in myself. Why wasn't I the type of woman that he could love through anything? Why wasn't I the kind of woman he wanted to hold onto for as long as possible?

I also felt a ton of shame. I was ashamed that I was so upset. I was ashamed that I was still hurt by our breakup long after it happened. I was ashamed every time someone asked about him or what happened to us—ashamed that I was single again despite all my efforts.

I had to sit with these feelings and honestly acknowledge what they meant. To get there, I had to go deeper. Going deeper took a ton of introspection. I asked myself question after question, and I did not shy away from the answers. I asked myself things like, Why does this bother me so much? Is this emotion linked to something I don't like about myself? Why do I resist this feeling? What does this mean if I feel this way? What would happen if I let go of this? Once you identify the specific emotion you are feeling, stay in that space, and look around. It's hard to see, but there is more to unearth just under the surface.

OFTEN, I WOULD STOP AND THINK I MUST HAVE BEEN CRAZY TO HAVE THIS MUCH LOVE FOR A PERSON WHO COULD END THINGS WITH ME SO CASUALLY.

EMOTION &
FEELING WHEEL

MAY THE FLOWERS
REMIND US WHY THE RAIN
IS SO NECESSARY
~ XAN OKU

Yes, your feelings are real and valid, but feelings are not facts. Feelings, like moods, are transient; they come and go and can always change. .

It is important to take a moment and take stock of what you are feeling. Self-awareness is one of the keys to healing your broken heart. You must first recognize what you are now feeling at this point in your journey. Knowing where you are will help guide you to where you want to end up eventually. Think of your feelings as a road map—each feeling guiding you to the next destination, ultimately leading you to where you want to be. For example, anger or sadness are easy feelings to recognize but push past just knowing you feel angry or sad and find the real feeling. It is in the knowing of what you really feel that will guide you to a more peaceful place.

"No matter how far life pushes you down, no matter how much you hurt, you can always bounce back." - Unknown

Allow yourself the space to get to the root of your feelings. Understanding our emotions is a crucial step towards our healing. Once we find and truly grasp the core emotions we are feeling, we can begin to empathize with ourselves and channel our focus in the direction of emotions we want to feel. The feeling wheel is so useful, because it enables you to visualize your emotions and understand the root of your pain. You can also use this feeling wheel to map out where you want to go emotionally. For example, if you want to feel joy, do something that makes you happy. If you want to feel love, find something you are passionate about.

Give yourself permission to be sad

Sadness is a fundamental human emotion. It's okay to be sad and feel sadness, especially when you have

been hurt or experienced a loss. Try to remember that being sad is a part of the human experience, and it is necessary to gauge how you should treat yourself. Be kind to yourself. Extend the same grace you would extend to a friend or loved one who is down. We may feel unnecessary pressure from society to be positive or put on a brave face, but it is okay to explore the feelings of sadness and figure out what you need at this moment. Since childhood, we have been trained that negative emotions or moods are a bad thing and should be eliminated as soon as possible. Well-intentioned friends and family will often attempt to help you feel better by encouraging you to 'cheer up' or to tell you to 'look on the bright side.' Just because sadness feels bad doesn't necessarily mean it is a bad emotion to have. If you feel the heavy weight of sadness coming on, take some time to acknowledge it and then push forward to something that feels better. You can't see it now, but this sadness will help you appreciate the happy moments that will surely come down the line.

6 Tips for Managing Sadness

- Allow yourself to be sad. Denying these feelings may force them underground, where they can do more harm than good. Cry if you need to. Notice if you feel relieved once you stop crying.

- Allow yourself ten minutes to cry or be sad. Ten minutes is usually a good length of time to start with, but feel free to adjust as needed.

- Write in your journal, listen to music, spend time with friends or family.

YOU CAN'T GET THE RELATIONSHIP YOU NEED FROM SOMEONE WHO IS NOT READY AND WILLING TO GIVE IT TO YOU

- Think about the root of the sad feelings. Refer back to the emotion and feeling wheel and try to figure out the specific emotion related to your sadness. Be kind to yourself as you work through your emotions.

- Don't overthink it. You don't need to analyze or do anything with your sadness. Just be willing to reflect on and express your sadness for five or ten minutes, then move on from it.

- Know when sadness has crossed over into depression. Get help if this happens rather than getting stuck in it. Depression can be debilitating for those that experience it. But there are many effective treatments available that can help you manage your depression symptoms.

According to the Mayo Clinic, "Depression is a mood disorder that causes a persistent feeling of sadness and loss of interest. Also called major depressive disorder or clinical depression, it affects how you feel, think, and behave and can lead to a variety of emotional and physical problems. You may have trouble doing normal day-to-day activities, and sometimes you may feel as if life isn't worth living.

More than just a bout of the blues, depression isn't a weakness, and you can't simply "snap out" of it. Depression may require long-term treatment. But don't get discouraged. Most people with depression feel better with medication, psychotherapy, or both." *Depression* (major depressive disorder)

If you think you might be depressed, talk with a doctor about how you're feeling. If you aren't ready to seek treatment, talk with a friend or loved one, or perhaps a trusted spiritual leader or minister. There is help available. You don't have to suffer in silence.

Signs of Depression

- Depressed mood (e.g. feeling sad or empty).

- Lack of interest in previously enjoyable activities.

- Significant weight loss or gain, a decrease or increase in appetite insomnia or hypersomnia.

- Agitation, restlessness, irritability.

- Fatigue or loss of energy.

- Feelings of worthlessness, hopelessness, and guilt, inability to think or concentrate, or indecisiveness.

- Recurrent thoughts of death, recurrent suicidal ideation, suicide attempt or plan. *Healthy ways to deal with sadness* (Gundersen Health System)

Release yourself from the guilt

Guilt is a useless emotion, and forgiveness is the cornerstone of healing. So forgive yourself. We are all human, and many times in this life, we will fall short of perfection. I know I have had my moments of being a little too clingy, a little too jealous, and other moments that were not exactly shining. But, I have also been kind and loving and patient when my partner wasn't their best either. It is easy to revisit and mentally rehash those moments and try and find ways that you are unlovable and unworthy, but I assure you, you are not. Set yourself free from those past regrets. That feeling that things could have turned out differently if only you had been better or behaved a certain way. We end up regretting the choices we make because we think we should have made other choices. We think we should have done something better, but we didn't, or we think we should have chosen a different path, but we didn't. We regret these choices, which are in the past and cannot be changed because we are comparing them to some nonexistent ideal path that we think we could have taken.

Now, if you are consistently repeating destructive behaviors, then it is time to take a look at yourself and assess why you are behaving this way. Most bad behavior and poor choices are rooted in fear of some sort (refer back to the emotion and feeling wheel). What is it that you are afraid of? Sometimes we act out in an effort to protect ourselves from something. Our brain tries to protect us from things we believe or feel are going to hurt us.

There is no need to feel guilty or regretful. This relationship is and was always meant to be a part of your growth, and you will grow from this. It may not feel like it now, but you will.

So release it.

Breakups, unfortunately, are like death, a mourning of a life you have only glimpsed. The future you envisioned with that person, the memories you planned to make have all died, and sometimes it comes suddenly and without warning to one of you. Once the shock has worn off, you have to release it. I know it hurts, but lean into it and allow yourself to feel it. Trust me, if anyone on this Earth has been lucky enough to experience love, then they have also likely experienced a similar heartbreak. It will be okay, you will be okay, you will survive this, and you will thrive again.

Make peace with what was, however beautiful, and know that it will never be again with that person.

Chapter 3| Feelings

Sticks and stones

We've all heard the old adage "Sticks and stones may break my bones, but words can never hurt me." Well, unfortunately, that saying isn't entirely accurate. Words hurt, they can cut deeply and leave scars that last a lifetime. During your breakup the other person may never say an unkind word about you. They may tell you something like, "It's not you; it's me." In this scenario, your ex likely didn't want to insult you or hurt your feelings. I once had a man tell me one of the reasons he didn't want to be with me was because I had accomplished nothing in the time that he had known me. Ouch! Here I was, a mother raising two lovely children, a homeowner with a great career who has lived a pretty awesome life full of travel and awesome adventures, and this person I respected so much, pretty much reduced me to nothing. It hurt, and I have to admit it threw me for a loop. Was it true? Was I this lazy person who had done nothing with their life? Looking back on it, I see how ridiculous it was to let those words bother me so much, but that is the thing with words. They have power, and they can hurt. Harsh words can be confusing, especially if they are coming from someone we love.

Try to remember that this person you love so much is also a flawed human being, prone to say or do anything in the midst of a breakup. Things can get ugly, or heated and they may say hurtful things that you had no idea they were feeling. Do your best to give those words little power over your life. Remember that your ex was likely hurting or angry in some way as well and could be looking to make you feel bad.

It helped me tremendously to categorize the things that were said to me. I asked myself these questions:

Was it honest? Honest words can be held up as a holy grail, and it is a truth that cannot be denied. There are factual truths in life, like what time someone arrived somewhere, or what you ate for dinner. There is also feedback, and feedback tends to be more of a perspective, which is each person's way of seeing things. So sometimes "being honest" is just giving an opinion.
For example, "you've accomplished nothing" is actually a perspective. From my ex's viewpoint, a lucrative career and numerous accolades are things he was always taught to strive for. On the other hand, I grew up in a large family where everyone gets married, has children, and buys a comfortable home. Having a comfortable home and family to return to at the end of the day is indeed a major accomplishment.

Was it criticism? Criticism is not the only truth, and it is merely one person's point of view, it is when we point out perceived flaws and mistakes in others. Criticism is usually intended to help someone improve, but it can feel like an "I'm right about this, and you are wrong" situation if given incorrectly. Criticism can leave you feeling down and resentful. In a previous relationship, I had a boyfriend who criticized the amount of time I spent at work. In his eyes, I prioritized work over spending time with him, but for me, I enjoyed the work I did, and I took great pride in doing a good job, no matter how long it took.

Chapter 3| Feelings

Was it constructive criticism? Constructive criticism is a little different and can be more useful than just criticism. Constructive criticism is when someone considers and fully understands all sides of a situation before offering their opinion. They consider the positives and negatives and make it clear they are only offering their take on things as they offer their viewpoints. Knowing that someone has considered all sides allows you to see ways forward, and to feel supported. Criticism can be useful if given fairly; oftentimes during a breakup we tend to forget this and receive everything negatively. Even constructive criticism can feel hurtful when this happens, even though the other person sees themselves as trying to help us.

Was it verbal abuse? With verbal abuse, the abuser intends to, whether they realize it or not, hurt and possibly control the person they offer their 'feedback' to. Verbal abuse, also sometimes called emotional abuse, also tends to criticize you as a person, not just what you did and the consequences of the action. And like all forms of abuse, verbal abuse is a way to take power over another by belittling or hurting them.

Some experts think verbal/Emotional abuse to be worse than physical abuse because the physical wounds can heal. In contrast, emotional abuse can have long term effects on the victim, some lasting a lifetime. If you find yourself questioning your perceptions, abilities, intuition, or gut feelings, or have low or no self-esteem. This may be an indicator of some sort of emotional abuse. If you think you have been the victim of abuse, contact the National Domestic Violence Hotline at https://www.thehotline.org/is-this-abuse/abuse-defined/ or (800) 799-7233/(800) 787-3224(TTY).

Don't allow anyone to tear you down with their words. Remember you are worthy of so much. You are worthy of happiness and positivity in a healthy relationship. You deserve to be treated with respect. You deserve it all.

Speak Kindness over yourself

Treat yourself like someone you love. Practice being your own best friend. How would you talk to a friend struggling through a breakup? No matter the circumstances of your breakup, now is the time to reassure yourself that you are worth being cared for. Love is still available to you. You are still enough, despite what may have been said or done to you. The inner dialogue you have with yourself is critical right now. Be kind and tolerant with yourself.

Challenge yourself to speak kindly to yourself during this time. You must let go of any negative messages from your ex. The more you dwell on and repeat any negative messages, the more your brain finds evidence to support them, and the more it begins to believe them, even if they were never true in the first place. Many of us have been conditioned to apologize and to beat ourselves up when someone speaks poorly of us, but it's possible to change that behavior. Speak kindness over your life! When you speak kindly to yourself on a consistent basis, you can experience higher levels of self-worth, more confidence, happiness, and less stress. Remember, there isn't a relationship in the world that is more important than the one you have with yourself.

Below are some examples of kind things you can say about yourself:

1. The world needs my light.
2. I am unique.
3. I can, and I will do something to promote healing in my life.
4. I can handle anything - one step at a time.
5. I deserve to be loved.
6. I am enough.
7. I get better every single day.
8. I love who I am.
9. I am proud of myself.
10. I am all the light I need.

Try the three activities below for the next week:

1. Every night for the next seven days, I want you to write three things you liked about yourself that day. They can be anything at all, big or small.

For example:
I felt confident when I made that important phone call.
I was patient with my children today.
I made time for myself today.

2. Ask people you trust to share what they like about you and what they think your strengths are. Even your children can give a valuable perspective. Write them down!

For example:
You are so resilient.
You have such good energy.
You make the best pancakes.

3. Write down any compliments you receive, no matter how big or small.

For example:
I'm so glad I know you.
You are a ray of sunshine.
I admire your courage.

KINDNESS

Use the space below to reinforce positive messages about yourself. Speak kindness over yourself. Remember to be your own best friend. It's okay to show yourself some compassion and understanding .

Write down three things you liked about yourself today.

Ask people to share what they like about you. Write it down!

Write down any compliments you receive. Big or small.

KINDNESS

Use the space below to reinforce positive messages about yourself. Speak kindness over yourself. Remember to be your own best friend. It's okay to show yourself some compassion and understanding .

Write down three things you liked about yourself today.

Ask people to share what they like about you. Write it down!

Write down any compliments you receive. Big or small.

KINDNESS

Use the space below to reinforce positive messages about yourself.
Speak kindness over yourself. Remember to be your own best friend.
It's okay to show yourself some compassion and understanding .

Write down three things you liked about yourself today.

Ask people to share what they like about you. Write it down!

Write down any compliments you receive. Big or small.

KINDNESS

Use the space below to reinforce positive messages about yourself.
Speak kindness over yourself. Remember to be your own best friend.
It's okay to show yourself some compassion and understanding .

Write down three things you liked about yourself today.

Ask people to share what they like about you. Write it down!

Write down any compliments you receive. Big or small.

Your Feelings

Use the Emotion and Feeling Wheel provided earlier to gain perspective into how you feel. Start with the core emotion and then dig deeper into what exactly it is you are feeling. Give your full attention to what you are feeling. Be gentle with yourself. Use the Emotion and Feeling Wheel to figure then where you want to go, and create a roadmap to get there.

How are you feeling right now?

How do you want to feel in 1 month? How will you get there?

How do you want to feel in 6 months? How will you get there?

Your Feelings

Use the Emotion and Feeling Wheel provided earlier to gain perspective into how you feel. Start with the core emotion and then dig deeper into what exactly it is you are feeling. Give your full attention to what you are feeling. Be gentle with yourself. Use the Emotion and Feeling Wheel to figure then where you want to go, and create a roadmap to get there.

How are you feeling right now?

How do you want to feel in 1 month? How will you get there?

How do you want to feel in 6 months? How will you get there?

Your Feelings

Use the Emotion and Feeling Wheel provided earlier to gain perspective into how you feel. Start with the core emotion and then dig deeper into what exactly it is you are feeling. Give your full attention to what you are feeling. Be gentle with yourself. Use the Emotion and Feeling Wheel to figure then where you want to go, and create a roadmap to get there.

How are you feeling right now?

How do you want to feel in 1 month? How will you get there?

How do you want to feel in 6 months? How will you get there?

Your Feelings

Use the Emotion and Feeling Wheel provided earlier to gain perspective into how you feel. Start with the core emotion and then dig deeper into what exactly it is you are feeling. Give your full attention to what you are feeling. Be gentle with yourself. Use the Emotion and Feeling Wheel to figure then where you want to go, and create a roadmap to get there.

How are you feeling right now?

How do you want to feel in 1 month? How will you get there?

How do you want to feel in 6 months? How will you get there?

28 DAYS UNDER THE SUN

THE HONOR PROMISE

Make a promise to honor yourself and everything you are feeling. Your feelings are valid, and your feelings matter. Be honest with yourself and what you are feeling. Don't be afraid of your feelings. Give yourself the same respect and love that you give to others. Allow yourself the space to feel and then heal.

THE ULTIMATE GUIDE TO HEALING FROM HEARTBREAK

I PROMISE TO...

honor my feelings. I will connect with my feelings, and make an effort to understand myself on a deeper level. I will be honest with what I feel and notice how I want to feel in the future. I will take action to feel better.

"

IN ORDER TO LOVE WHO YOU ARE, YOU CANNOT HATE THE EXPERIENCES THAT SHAPED YOU.

~ Andrea Dykstra

CHAPTER

HOW TO STOP
THE HURT

"SOMETIMES IT TAKES AN OVERWHELMING BREAKDOWN TO HAVE AN UNDENIABLE BREAKTHROUGH. " ~ UNKNOWN

As the days and weeks continued to pass, I knew I needed to do something else to push myself through the sadness. Although I still checked my phone pretty regularly for a text or missed call from him, I had pretty much given up hope that he would come running back to me, and I wanted some relief, so I joined a gym. The gym was a pleasant change from going to work and then straight to my bed. I knew endorphins were real, and I wanted to put myself in a position to feel something good, anything other than the weight of the sadness I had been feeling. I bought some cute workout gear, nothing expensive, but something to make me feel nice when I went to the gym.

On my first day at the gym, I took a spin class. I wasn't new to working out and had worked out consistently many times in my life, but like many people, I fell off once I found myself head over heels in love. I'm one of those people who loves spending all of my free time with my partner. The downside of that is it makes it easy to lose parts of ourselves. And while it is important to spend time together, it is also important to maintain your individuality and do the things you enjoy.

Spin class was familiar, and I always enjoyed it, so I started there. The music that first day kind of sucked, and when the instructor played one particularly cheesy song about breaking up and moving on, the flood gates opened and I cried. Thankfully it was dark, and wiping tears can be mistaken for wiping sweat, so no one noticed. When class was over, I sat in the sauna for 20 minutes and cried a little more.

I was still sad, but there was also another feeling

there. I felt accomplished. It wasn't happiness or joy, but it was something other than sadness, and that was really all I needed at the moment. I decided to chase that feeling.

You have a choice.

I realized after that spin class that I had a choice. I could choose to continue being sad. I could continue to spend days and weeks feeling sorry for myself, sinking further and further into the fog of sadness and self-pity. Or I could do something else. My decision to feel better was mine to make, and it was the pivotal moment in healing my broken heart. I decided that I was not a powerless victim who just had to wait for time to heal my wounds. I could take willful action to heal my broken heart. And you can too.

Deciding that you are ready to heal is the number one way you end the pain you are experiencing. Actively pursuing healing and committing to feeling better is the key. It is in your commitment to yourself that you will find peace. Show up for yourself every day. Commit and recommit to working through the healing process as many times as you need to. Let go of any beliefs you hold about what needs to happen for you to heal.

These are simply thoughts that keep you distracted from healing. You do not need an apology. You do not need closure. Your healing is your responsibility alone. You are not some passive, powerless victim, waiting for words or actions from someone else to feel better. Once you decide to heal from heartbreak, every action you take will support that decision.

Be courageous. Healing is hard work. Your ex and your breakup, though painful, are very familiar to you. Stepping into the unknown can be scary, but you are not bound to your past. Your breakup is now a part of your past. Heal yourself by refusing to look backward. We are living in the present, always moving forward. Your joy is here and now, and all we have is this moment.

Pro tip: I'm a crier. If I'm really upset, I can get all worked up and start crying. I once found myself just sitting and sobbing about my breakup. I was sitting in my room crying so much, just feeling very sad and miserable, and then the thought hit me. Here I was alone in my house. No one was there physically harming me. My ex was not on the other end of the phone saying anything to me. No nasty text messages were being sent. The only reason I

was crying was due to the thoughts in my mind. I was replaying old conversations or imagining my ex being happy somewhere without me. I was sad about something that had happened in the past, or things that I didn't even know to be true. It then dawned on me that I could stop crying. I could shift the focus of those thoughts and focus solely on what was currently happening, which was nothing. There was no real reason for me to be crying about those things. So I just stopped. I pushed all of those thoughts of old conversations and old things that had happened out of my mind. The next time you find yourself all worked up and crying about your ex, take a moment, and access what is happening around you. If you are physically safe and just going over past events or future events that you don't even know to be true. Just stop. Breathe and place your focus somewhere else.

Do things that give you back some sense of power and control over your life. The following steps were essential to my healing process. After I made the conscious decision to heal my broken heart. These activities renewed my sense of purpose and allowed me to focus on something more than just heartache.

Find a good feeling and chase it

Ask yourself: what makes you feel good? If the answer to this question comes easily, then go and find that thing and do it. If the answer doesn't come to you as easily, then it is time to do some inner work and exploration. The world is vast, and there are many things you can experiment with and learn that will bring you a feeling of joy and peace. It can be something as simple as a walk through nature or as big as running a 10k and feeling a sense of accomplishment. Be mindful during this time not to indulge in unhealthy activities that may feel good for a moment, but ultimately jeopardize your health — both mentally and physically.

The Joy of Small Things

It may not feel like it now, but there is still joy. Remember the small things you enjoy, like reading a good book or laughing with a friend. There is something to be said about spending a Sunday afternoon getting lost in the pages of a great novel or cooking yourself a good meal. You may not be the best cook, but find a recipe and spend some time with yourself, creating something delicious. Make it pretty, and savor what you have created. Treasure the memories you make doing these small things you enjoy and revisit these memories from time to time.

Make time

Carve out time to do something for yourself, no matter how small. Make it something you can look forward to. I once scheduled a walk around my neighborhood. Such a small thing, but when you are in the midst of a traumatic situation, having something to look forward to can really make you feel better. So as I looked for ways to improve my mood, I scheduled this walk. I picked a beautiful Saturday afternoon, and I decided I would walk as far as I could for an hour and then turn around. I planned the time and what I would wear, and I decided that as I was walking, I would take the time to be grateful for every blessing in my life. I decided to spend that hour honoring all the good things in this world and my life. As I walked, I began to remember that life was still good and full and beautiful. In that hour, it became clear that even though I was hurting, the seasons were still changing as they have my entire life. The sun still rose in the east and set in the west. And I was still amazing, and worthy, and as lovable as I had ever been.

Volunteer

Volunteering is another great way to feel good about yourself and bring joy back into your life. Volunteering has been shown to provide a healthy boost to your self-confidence, self-esteem, and overall life satisfaction. It can positively impact your community and can also help you brush up on your social skills by connecting you to new friends. You can even volunteer on a small-scale, like helping a friend or neighbor in need. I once volunteered with an organization that made lunch bags and handed them out one afternoon to people in need. It was nice to meet some new people and to have small tasks like making sandwiches to focus on. It was small in terms of effort and time commitment, but the appreciation I felt from the recipients of those lunches was incredible. Volunteering provided a reminder that I am needed in this world and I have the ability to make a difference.

Look for ways in which you can make a difference in your local community.

Set some goals

Having a goal to accomplish helps tremendously to take your mind off of your relationship status. What are some of the things you would like to accomplish, but never had the time to do? Now is your chance. Goals are a part of our long term vision for our lives. Goals help us define where it is we are going. Once we establish that vision for ourselves, we can then align our actions towards that end goal. Goals are vital. They create markers in our lives. Do you want a life that happens at random? Or do you want to live your life by design? If you answered by design, then now is the perfect time to firmly place those goals in your mind and work towards them. You are capable of achieving greatness, even at this moment. Even though things might feel bleak, you got this! There are so many great moments and achievements still out there waiting for you. All you need is the willingness to dedicate the time to your goals and a bit of persistence, and you will get there.

Good things rarely just happen to people at random; you must make a plan, figure out a way to make it happen, and be consistent. Remember that you've got a real good shot at some pretty great things, especially right now. So sign up for that course, train for that race, maybe even write that book. Channel everything you've got into your goals and make yourself proud!

AND I WAS STILL AMAZING, AND WORTHY, AND AS LOVABLE AS I HAD EVER BEEN.

THE HEALING PROMISE

Make a promise today to commit to healing your broken heart. You will actively pursue healing and commit yourself to feeling better. You will dedicate yourself to that healing by participating in activities that make you feel good. You will set new goals, make time for yourself, look for happiness in life's small details.

I PROMISE TO...

heal. I commit myself to healing from this heartbreak. I will commit and recommit to the healing process as many times as I need. I am living in the moment and not obsessing over the past. I will not worry about things I have no control over. I will find things that bring me joy. And I will focus on things that make me happy.

> Closure is an illusion, the winking of the eye of a storm. Nothing is completely resolved in life, nothing is perfect. The important thing is to keep living because only by living can you see what happens next.
>
> ~ Patti Smith

CHAPTER

05

MOVING ON

THEY WON'T FIND SOMEONE BETTER THAN YOU, THEY WILL FIND SOMEONE BETTER FOR THEM, AND YOU WILL TOO...AND IN TIME YOU WILL REALIZE THAT IT IS OKAY.

Today a friend posted pictures of a party that took place over the weekend. I always like this friend's pictures; he is a professional photographer and takes great photos at events all over the city. I scrolled through the photos and was surprised to come across my ex and his new girlfriend. I felt awful, and all the pain came rushing back at once. I spent more time than I care to admit looking at those pictures, trying to see answers that would never be there. I wondered what was so great about this woman? Did he find her prettier than me? Kinder? Nicer? Does she have something that I don't have? Is he happier? I knew repeatedly looking at these pictures would bring me no peace, just more questions, but I couldn't help myself.

Later, I found myself typing out a long text to my ex and I seriously contemplated pressing send What happened? I had been doing so well. No creeping on his social media, no contact, and yet there he was in a picture on a random friend's Facebook page, and it sent me into a tailspin.

I realized that day that it was time to move on. Moving on is hard, but you can get there. We've already mentally let this person go, but we now want to be able to see and interact with them and be okay. Think about when you leave one job and go to a new one. You are no longer thinking about or concerned with your old workplace. If they hire someone new to do your old job, it's not your concern anymore.You don't work there. If the new person sucks or flourishes at your old job, it doesn't matter. You may hear it through the grapevine, or people may mention the new person your ex is dating to you in passing,but this information should have zero effect on you or your well being. I most certainly struggled when it came time to move on from my ex, but I found tools to help me get to the other side.

Comparison

Don't compare yourself to anyone else. If you find yourself in that place: stop immediately!

I know it's hard not to study this new partner; and make unnecessary comparisons, but this new partner your ex has found is no better than you. We all have gifts, and we all bring value to those around us. If you somehow get caught up comparing yourself to the new partner, I want you to stop, take a deep breath, and then mentally list ten remarkable things about yourself. Think of ten things that have nothing to do with anyone else. For example, instead of saying, "I'm a great mom/dad," try to list something solely about you and don't rely on things you do for other people. For me, I have a great smile and a walk that can rival any supermodel on Earth!

Maybe you tell great jokes or make a great lasagna. Remember those things about yourself and how unique and admirable these qualities make you. It's easy to get down on yourself by comparing yourself to the next man or woman, but there are some great traits and qualities about yourself that

would make the next person green with envy. Dig into those things, remember who you were before this relationship, and remember the great person you will always be.

Boundaries

Occasionally, it's okay to stay friends with an ex. Some great friendships have been born from ex's, but in this instance, space will be needed. During a major breakup, I know you want nothing more than to stay in your ex's life, to keep tabs on what they are doing and who they are seeing, but this will do more harm than good. Your ex may even really want to stay a part of your life, and you may not want to be seen as "the bad guy" or bitter. It really is best to create some clear boundaries. Setting boundaries is you determining what you want to do with your time and space. Let's say your ex invites you to a family function because their mom or sisters still love you. You don't have to go if you aren't ready. You do not have to answer when they call you (this boundary may look different if you are co-parenting). You do not have to allow them in your home or living area. You get to determine what the boundaries are for you specifically. You both need time and space to heal from the end of your relationship. Remember that your healing is not their responsibility and vice versa. It may be difficult at first to not see or speak to your

I PROMISE YOU THERE ARE SOME GREAT TRAITS AND QUALITIES ABOUT YOURSELF THAT WOULD MAKE THE NEXT PERSON GREEN WITH ENVY!

ex, but these boundaries will help six months down the line when one of you may be feeling lonely or sad or bored and want to use the other to soothe whatever ails them.

Social Media

Beware of social media and the deception that it may contain. We've all posted pictures and moments in time that have had nothing to do with what is actually going on in our lives at that moment. Do not believe everything you see. Understand that people post pretty pictures when they are feeling down and smiling pictures when they are crying inside. Don't get caught up in the memes or smiling videos posted by your ex. In fact, as you are healing, it's best to take a break from viewing their social media. I prefer to unfriend instead of mute, but no matter how you get there, it is important to protect your peace by not viewing their page or stories. Refrain from posting things of your own aimed at sending a message to your ex or your mutual friends. You may also find it beneficial to delete any photos of the two of you from your social media accounts. If you can't do it right away, it's okay, but at some point, you are going to have to remove them from your accounts if you are struggling to get over them. Revisiting old memories over and over again will do nothing but delay your healing.

PRO TIP: Phone a friend. Anytime you want to call your ex, call a friend, or your mom, or your dad. Do not call your ex. And for God's sake, do not send that text! If you have no one else to call, pull out your journal, and write your thoughts and feelings down. Leave everything on those pages. Do not give in to your feelings at this moment. These feelings will pass.

Love Yourself

I know it sounds downright odd to have to say this, but LOVE yourself. We spend lots of time in relationships learning all we can about our partners and finding ways to show them how much we love and care for them. Use this time to love on yourself. Take a good look at yourself, both physically and spiritually. Recognize the beauty that is uniquely yours. Honestly, you have your own gifts, strengths, talents, and experiences. There is no one else like you who can give the world exactly what you have to offer. You are rare. Like the Mona Lisa or a Jackson Pollock, remember that you are literally irreplaceable, a one of one. Use this space in your life to be a bit selfish and focus solely on you. Take the same love and care that you would show to a partner and do things that will benefit you.

Isolation

Be mindful of isolation. Often we go through things in life, and we feel embarrassed. Embarrassment can lead to guilt and shame.

That shame can cause us to isolate ourselves from others. We sometimes end up feeling alone in our problems and come to the belief that it's better to turn inward than to share with the people who love us the most. I can assure you that there is nothing to be embarrassed about. Every human being on this Earth has faced trials and tribulations. You may feel that no one will understand your pain, but I guarantee you this isn't true. Isolating yourself from family and friends may end up having an adverse effect. Find someone you can share your thoughts and feelings with, whether it be a trusted friend or counselor, or perhaps an online group for people going through a similar situation. It will feel good to talk and share with others.

Support (Family & Friends)

It is a loss, a tremendous loss, and it is okay to lean on the people closest to you as you find your way to some sense of normalcy. Leaning doesn't have to mean pouring your heart out and telling everyone what a jerk your ex was and how he/she is missing out on the best thing that ever happened to them. Sometimes leaning on someone is just going for a walk and talking about a new movie you plan to see, or grabbing a bite and catching up on old times. Giving and receiving support from others is a basic human need, one you shouldn't shy away from. We all need a support system that will laugh with us, cry with us, and hold our hands while we go through life's ups and downs.

Revenge

My mother once told me, "the best revenge is a life well-lived." And that is what you must do. There is absolutely no need to try to exact some form of revenge on your ex. Sure it may feel good for a moment to damage their property or slander them on social media or call the H.R. department of their job and report their misappropriation of office supplies. But what would that accomplish? Nothing my friend, absolutely nothing. All it will do is prove to people on the outside looking in that your ex made the correct decision in getting away from your crazy self.

You do not need revenge.

You do not need to warn the next person about them or anyone for that matter.

You do not need to explain your side of the story or try to convince their friends and family how awful of a person your ex is.

You do not need to do any of these things or any variation of these things.

You only need to heal. Turn that fire inward and use it to light your own path to greatness.

Once upon a time, I went through the most devastating breakup of my life, instead of focusing on him, I shifted my focus inward, and I pushed myself to write a book about it. When my heart was broken, I never imagined that I would find the strength to rise up and triumph over my pain. Through a commitment to my own growth, I was able to find powerful ways to reframe my pain into a new self-awareness.

There is a path that can transform heartache into a new chapter in life. And it begins with you. Whether you funnel that pain into a bestselling book, a master's degree, or a revenge body, put some purpose behind that pain and come out on the other side better than you have ever been!

THE ONWARD PROMISE

Moving on from a relationship is a decision.
Make a promise to yourself to move for good.
The energy it takes to hold on to the past will
prevent you from moving on and connecting
with new people. As we move on, we
acknowledge the lessons and the growth that
came from the old relationship, and allow
better opportunities to present themselves in
the future.

I PROMISE TO...

move on. I am no longer affected by the relationships in my past. I am looking forward to new opportunities, new people and new energy. I am taking the time to love myself.

CHAPTER

DIGNITY

"KNOWING WHEN TO WALK AWAY IS WISDOM. BEING ABLE TO, IS COURAGE. WALKING AWAY WITH YOUR HEAD HELD HIGH IS DIGNITY"
-UNKNOWN

Many moons ago, I was a young woman with a hot temper going through a divorce. Divorce is never easy. My ex and I were on decent terms, and one Saturday afternoon, he was running late to pick up our daughters for the weekend. I called him to get an idea of the time he would be arriving. He told me he got caught up and was running behind. He was still at home and would come to my house to pick up the girls in the next hour or so. I was already heading out, and thought, why don't I help him by delivering the girls right to his doorstep. In my mind, this felt like a sweet gesture, and I was more than ready for some me time. We had a good co-parenting relationship, and it was important to me for that to continue. So I drove the 15 minutes to his house and knocked on the door. He seemed a bit surprised to see me, but he thanked me for

dropping them off and ushered the girls inside. Once back in the car, I noticed my youngest daughter had forgotten her game that she had been playing with.

I rushed back up to the house and knocked on the door. My daughters answered. They looked at me nervously as I handed my youngest her game. "Is everything okay?" I asked curiously. They quickly looked from me to back inside the house. I could tell something was up. "Is someone in there?" I asked. They answered "Yes." in unison. "Is it a lady?" I continued. They both looked at me, neither said a word. I could tell they were afraid to answer. By this time, their father returned to the door. "Do you have a woman in there?" I demanded. He looked at me, then looked at our girls and softly replied, "Yes." I could feel my blood starting to boil. Yes, we were *separated. Yes, he had every right to entertain anyone he wanted, but it felt so soon. It hurt to have evidence of him moving on with his life without me. I know we agreed to separate, but how dare there be another woman here, around my family. I wanted to push past the three of them and run inside. I wanted to give this woman a piece of my mind and let her know that she could never replace me. I wanted to make my presence known to this woman and let her know that I was the Queen Bee. But I looked down, and there were my daughters, still watching the exchange between their dad and me. I took a breath, and instead of causing a scene, I turned and walked back to my car. I decided right then to maintain my dignity. I decided that maintaining my dignity was more important than my ego. I realized I have no control over what others choose to do with their lives or their time. I remembered that the only person I can control is myself. And so I did.*

We tend to think that there is nothing worse than being rejected by the one we love, but what's even more damaging than losing the one you love is losing yourself to someone who doesn't want you. I want you to think about your dignity. Dignity is defined as a sense of pride in oneself, and it is directly tied to our value and worth as human beings.

Dignity is the recognition that we are worthy of good things. So if you find yourself being dumped or rejected by your partner, I want you to keep your dignity at the forefront of your mind. Your dignity is yours, and it cannot be taken away from you, but you can throw it away (as I almost did). It may not feel very important now, but six months, twelve months, two years down the line when you look back at this breakup, you will be happy to have kept your dignity. Imagine a time way in the future. You are out and about, looking and feeling good. You run into your ex. Will you shrink back, hoping not to be seen, because the last memory they have of you is you screaming at the top of your lungs about something trivial. Or will you walk by with confidence, with your self-respect intact? Knowing you have and will always operate in a space of grace, honor, and dignity. I know things may be unpleasant at this moment, but keeping your dignity and handling things with grace and maturity now will feel so much better in the long run.

There may come a time during the breakup that you see (whether in person or through social media) or hear that your ex has moved on to someone new. This information may cause you to experience many feelings, ranging from jealousy to anger to sadness and hurt.

WHAT'S EVEN MORE DAMAGING THAN LOSING THE ONE YOU LOVE IS LOSING YOURSELF TO SOMEONE WHO DOESN'T WANT YOU.

Chapter 6 | Dignity

You may get the urge to confront your ex or even contact their new partner to warn them. Do not do it!

Contacting your ex or their new partner will in no way make you feel better. There are no answers you can receive that will make you feel better; nothing can come from this but more hurt on your end. Having dignity is having respect for yourself as well as others.

Make that Promise to yourself right here and now. No matter what comes, you will keep yourself calm and handle all situations without compromising your self-respect. Your relationship has ended. but that doesn't mean your pride and self-respect have to leave with it.

"

IF IT'S MEANT FOR YOU, YOU WONT HAVE TO BEG FOR IT. YOU WILL NEVER HAVE TO SACRIFICE YOUR DIGNITY FOR YOUR DESTINY.

~ Edgar Allen Poe

THE DIGNITY PROMISE

Make a promise to yourself to keep your dignity at all times and through all things. Even if you find yourself having to interact with your ex, and they are choosing to act a complete fool. You will continue to hold your head as high as you can. You will remember this Promise and remove yourself from the situation as quickly and as safely as possible.

I PROMISE TO...

keep my dignity at all times and through all things. No matter what comes, I will remain calm and handle all situations with grace and dignity. Never compromising my self-respect,

CHAPTER

07

THE STORM

STOP TRYING TO CALM THE STORM, CALM YOURSELF,
THE STORM WILL PASS.

A storm hit today. I never saw it coming. It's been months since we last spoke or even saw each other. I still think about you often, but not nearly as much as I used to. Today though, you were everywhere, in every thought formed and every image in my mind. I try now to only think about the bad things in our relationship, and there were plenty, but that isn't stopping this pain. When we were dating, I felt so connected to you that I even knew when you were going to call. It's as if I could tell when I was on your mind. As our relationship was coming to an end, I couldn't feel you anymore. Today, I felt you. I felt you, especially as I cried myself to sleep.

Emotions can sometimes rush in like storms, catching you off guard.

If you find yourself in the midst of an emotional storm, you must do what you can to push through.

You must decide not to act or react out of emotion. Just because you wake up thinking about your ex does not mean you should reach out to them. Sometimes in these moments, you look for any reason to make contact again... DON'T. Sometimes a random dream about someone is just that; it isn't a sign that they are thinking of you, or a push from God or the Universe to give them a call. In these moments, it is best just to be still and let them pass.

Chapter 7| The Storm

As I worked through my breakup, I discovered the power of meditation. There is tremendous power in stillness and harnessing your mind's ability to block out thoughts and consciously focus on nothingness. Through meditation, I was able to navigate these moments of powerlessness. When I wanted nothing more than to contact my ex and just yell at him one more time or demand an explanation for him hurting me like this, meditation allowed me to just be still. I would find a quiet place to sit, set a ten-minute timer on my phone, and just focus on breathing. Breathing was all that mattered in those ten minutes. Thoughts would come, and I would let them, but I would not hold on to them, I would simply let them go. The only thing I held onto was the focus on my breath.

How will you handle these storms that will surely come? Will you face them head-on? Will you stand strong or allow the winds to toss you around like yesterday's trash?.

The greater your storm, the brighter your rainbow.

The next time you find yourself in the midst of a storm, I want you to try a simple meditation. This meditation aims to calm the mind, which will help you navigate any storms that may come your way. It takes practice, but meditation might be simpler than you think.

Find a place where you can relax into this process, set a timer, and give it a try:

1) Find a space - Find a place to sit or lay down that feels calm and quiet.

2) Set a time limit - If you're just beginning, it can help to set a short timer on your phone. I started with ten minutes.

3) Notice your body - You can sit in a chair with your feet on the floor, you can sit cross-legged, or you can lie down. All of these positions will work; just be sure to be comfortable.

4) Focus on your breath - Close your eyes and follow the sensation of your breath as it goes in and as it goes out. Breath in...Breath out.

5) Notice when your mind has wandered - Naturally, your attention will leave the breath and wander to other places. When you notice that your mind has wandered, practice letting go. Guide your thoughts back to your breathing. There is no need to hold on to any thoughts. Your only focus right now is your breath. Breath in....Breath out.

6) End with kindness - When you're ready, gently open your eyes. Take a moment and notice the sights and sounds around you. Notice how your body feels right now. Notice your thoughts and emotions.

Smile. You did it.

That's it. You can practice this simple meditation daily, or use it when you find yourself having trouble staying calm. Remember, there is strength in your stillness.

"

TO THE MIND THAT IS STILL, THE WHOLE UNIVERSE SURRENDERS

~ Lao Tzu

THE STILLNESS PROMISE

Expect that storms will come. Recognize when you are in the midst of an emotional storm. You cannot control the storm. You can only control yourself. Be still. Allow the storm to pass. Do not allow chaos and destruction to wreak havoc in your life.

I PROMISE TO...

get still when the storms of life begin to rage. I will find a safe space and focus only on my breath. I know there is strength and power in stillness, and I will use this power as needed.

CHAPTER

SOBRIETY

08

"SOBRIETY IS NOT A LIMITATION, IT'S A SUPERPOWER"
-BRENE BROWN

I once had a guy dump me in the rudest way. We had been an official 'couple' for about a week, and I had a family emergency and had to go to the hospital. I called him to reschedule our date for later that evening, and to my surprise, he didn't believe me. He accused me of lying and unceremoniously dumped me over the phone and then proceeded to block my number. I was shocked. I tried unsuccessfully to reach him because I knew that there had to be some type of misunderstanding on his part, but we never really spoke again. Having my new relationship end abruptly that way stung. I was more hurt about being accused of lying than I was about him ending the relationship.

I went out the following weekend with my girlfriends and honestly drank way too much.

I guess I wanted to prove something that night, maybe that I was still fun, still desirable. Perhaps I had hoped that he would see pictures of me living it up on social media and feel like a fool and beg to have me back in his life. Or maybe I wanted him to hurt like I was hurt. I honestly don't even remember what I wanted anymore. In any event, I'm almost positive I acted a drunken fool that night (thank God for girlfriends who love you). Overdoing it that night was not only dangerous, but it accomplished nothing. I woke up the next morning with very little memory of the night before and a massive headache.

Chapter 8 | Sobriety

In hindsight, I am 100% sure that this man did me a huge favor by dumping me. I had no business being in a relationship with a man who could be neither kind nor compassionate when I needed it most.

There is no denying that heartbreak is painful. In my experience, heartbreak can sometimes feel like someone is physically ripping your heart out of your chest. In these moments, you may find yourself searching for something, anything to numb the pain. Turning to drugs or alcohol in an attempt to feel better is not the answer. When we are hurting and vulnerable, it's easy to pour yourself a few extra glasses of wine or do a few more tequila shots than you usually would, but these things won't help you in the long run.

The use or overuse of these substances is merely a distraction, a delaying of the inevitable healing process that you desperately need to go through. Remember my dear, that the only way out is through.

As you are in this space of healing, be mindful of drug and alcohol usage. Something that may temporarily ease the pain you are in can easily lead you to make bad decisions that you may regret later down the line.

THE SOBRIETY PROMISE

Make a promise to yourself today to remain sober until you are through the worst of this breakup. A clear mind will help you make better decisions and not slip up and send cringe-worthy drunk texts that you will regret once the sun comes up. Or worse, lead you into the arms of the person who broke your heart only to have them restart the heartbreak clock the next morning.

I PROMISE TO...

remain sober until I can see clearly
during this breakup. I will not
attempt to dull the pain through
outside substances.
The only way out is through.

VALUE YOUR VALUE

"YOUR VALUE DOESN'T DECREASE BASED ON SOMEONE'S INABILITY TO SEE YOUR WORTH." ~UNKNOWN

One weekend, I was feeling particularly down. I was sad and deep in my feelings about being dumped. I decided to stay in my bedroom, isolated from the world. I was having a good old-fashioned pity party, and I was the proud guest of honor. From my bedroom, though, I could hear my daughters go on about their lives, talking, making dinner, coming, and going. On Sunday evening, when I felt better, I finally emerged from my room to spend time with them. As I entered the living room, I could feel the energy shift. This shift was something I had never really noticed before. The mood seemed to brighten, and I felt a calmness and warming from my girls. As we began talking and catching up on the weekend events, I could see the positive effects of my presence on them. At that moment, it hit me—I'm adding value just by showing up. Just by being myself and chatting with my girls, I was having a positive effect on them. It was clear to me that things were different and better, simply because I was present. I gave more thought to how their lives would be if I simply disappeared. I then began paying attention to the effect my presence had in other everyday situations. By expressing my silly, sometimes goofy, genuine self, I realized that I positively impacted people. I was sending out positive energy by just showing up. This phenomenon had been happening my entire life, but I hadn't always noticed it. Over time, as this idea took root in my mind, I began to truly understand the value that I brought to the world around me. The value that I added to everyone I encountered.

We all have something unique and valuable to give to the world. Some people contribute in small ways, some contribute in substantial ways, but everyone's contribution is important. You are you for a reason. Your quirks, your idiosyncrasies, the things that make you unique and who you are exist for a purpose. You are valuable, and you are worthy. Worthy of love, safety, and security. Deserving of a love that doesn't come with pain. You deserve more than just being tolerated. You have an inherent right to exist in the world around you. It is not a right that you have to earn. You are just as worthy as any other person.

What do you think you are worth? Imagine for a moment your most expensive, most amazing, fabulous material possession, be it a really nice watch or an expensive pair of shoes. Now imagine a stranger on the street walking up to you and pulling out a crumpled up one-dollar bill and offering that to you in exchange for that material item that you really treasure. You would be offended, and you'd never settle for anything less than what you believe your precious item is worth. Now apply that logic to yourself and your own personal value. I personally have known people with amazing talents and gifts who

were, for some reason settling for relationships and circumstances where they clearly were not being valued.

It begins with your self-worth.

You don't have to settle for a $1 relationship or a $1 anything for that matter. You would be surprised at how quickly things will change for you the moment you realize who you really are and the value you truly have to offer to another human being. It's time for you to seek out and recognize places and situations where your presence makes a significant difference. Exercise self-love. Who and what you allow into your life paints a vivid picture of the love you have for yourself.

Life has tricked many of us into humbling ourselves and dimming our own light. Too many of us are walking through life, believing that we are ordinary. And that in order to be loved and liked, we have to fit into some box and be more like everyone else. The truth is that you alone are special and uniquely made. The you that you are today, right at this moment, is needed in this world. The more you try to fit into some made-up ideal, the more you diminish your own light. Take back ownership of your self-worth. There is a reason we call it self-worth.

point of view.
Value [val´ū·] *n.*
property of a th
useful or estim
ᵃsonable pri

YOU WOULD BE SURPRISED AT HOW QUICKLY THINGS WILL CHANGE FOR YOU THE MOMENT YOU REALIZE WHO YOU REALLY ARE, AND THE VALUE YOU TRULY HAVE TO OFFER TO ANOTHER HUMAN BEING.

Chapter 9 | Value your value

Decide today that you and only you determine your value. You will no longer allow the thoughts and actions of others to validate you. You control your self-worth, and the decisions you make going forward will reflect the high value you have put on yourself. Be confident and clear about how amazing you are and what a genuine gift you are to this world. Recognize, celebrate, and love the parts of yourself that make you special, unique, and different.

Take inventory of your gifts, talents, and unique life experiences. Embrace them and be grateful for the richness they have added to your life. You have already overcome so much that has brought you to where you are now in your life. Fully recognize the wins and achievements you've already experienced. Step back and look at your strengths and weaknesses from a new perspective. We all have strengths and weaknesses. As you begin to see yourself clearly, the secret is to lean into and maximize your strengths and not allow your weaknesses to define you. You can honor and benefit from both.

It begins with your Self-Worth.

When it comes to seeing and evaluating yourself, many people tend to do the opposite of what is most rewarding. They are quick to diminish their strengths and emphasize their weaknesses, making themselves feel as though they aren't good enough. Do not allow your weaknesses to determine your value. Instead, you must know that you are unique with something precious to give the world. Lean into your strengths and learn to use your weaknesses as opportunities to grow.

You are an amazing person, and your life is already worth more than you can imagine. It's time to see the value in who you truly are, and not through the distorted lens of what others think and say about you, but through a self-aware and empowered lens that shows you truth and real perspective. And, as you fully embrace yourself as you are, you will step into a higher level of self-worth as the master of your own life. Remember, this is your life. You live life once, so don't live it playing small or looking at it through a lens of diminished value. The truth is that you are valuable and have something incredible to give the world.

So, go out there, live your life to the fullest.

Pro tip - Growth not only happens when you are winning in life, it happens when things are not going well. Trust in your strengths and look for ways to use them to expand yourself.

THE VALUE PROMISE

Promise yourself to remember your value. It
doesn't matter what anyone has said about
you. They don't determine your value, you do.
Starting today you are noticing that you
make a difference just by showing up. You
are noticing your strengths and embracing
who you are right at this moment. Your value
isn't delayed or based on something that
hasn't happened yet. It's right here right now.

I PROMISE TO...

value my value. I know my worth and I claim my value. I will move through life, knowing I am worthy of love and respect. I add value to every room that I enter and every space that I occupy. I deserve to be treated with consideration and respect, and I will operate in this space at all times.

"

DON'T YOU KNOW YET? IT IS YOUR LIGHT THAT LIGHTS THE WORLD.

~ RUMI

CHAPTER

THE LIGHT

"IF LIGHT IS IN YOUR HEART YOU WILL FIND YOUR WAY HOME."
- RUMI

It had been months since my breakup. It was late August, my favorite time of the year. Long days, and warm nights, usually filled with days at the pool and barbecues and brunch with friends and family. Lately, though, I had just been working and coming right home. One evening, as I was winding down, the newscaster's smooth yet perky voice caught my attention. She was going on and on about the fact that it had been sunny for twenty-eight straight days, and how wonderful it had been.

"Twenty-eight bright, beautiful days under the sun." She remarked. Her comment stopped me dead in my tracks. Hmph, I thought. Here I was getting up and going through life's motions day after day, and I hadn't even noticed that it had been sunny for twenty-eight straight days.

When my breakup was fresh in the spring, I not only noticed the rain, I almost looked forward to it?

Every day it rained, I took notice and even felt as if the rain was the world crying right along with me. But here I was months later, barely noticing the Sun's glorious warmth beaming down on me for twenty-eight days straight. How could this be?! How was it that I hadn't even noticed? Was I so determined to be sad that I couldn't recognize anything else? I walked toward my bedroom window. That same window, I set my eyes to back on that fateful day in the Spring As I raised the blinds, the light from the Sun began to wash over me. Twenty-eight days under the Sun, I thought. i instantly knew that I didn't want to let any more *days go by, not recognizing that light. I thought about how important the Sun is, it warms our seas and stirs our skies. It is the giver of life for many things and provides light, warmth, and direction for those who need to find their way. I decided at that moment that I would turn towards that light. Not only would I turn to it, but I would look for it every day of my life, and on the days when there was cloud cover or rain, I decided I would be the light.*

In life, there are guaranteed to be storms. There will be moments and endings and events that will change you and the way you see the world. I say, let them. Let these moments shape you. Let them make you stronger and kinder and smarter and everything in between. The world can, at times, be dark and chaotic. It is our duty to find the sun when it is missing from our sky. We must fight to keep our inner sunshine alive. Storms will blow through our lives, and we will grow to understand that we can't always control the weather, but we must cultivate and defend our inner conditions. We must learn to take the sunshine with us wherever we go.

We all have an inner light, that internal sunshine that shines within each and every one of us. When we are born, that light is glowing and powerful; its warmth embraces and draws people in. As we go through our lives, our light becomes shaded by disappointments, and the responsibilities and expectations of daily life.

Although it may seem to dull over time, your light will always be within your reach. That inner light is always there, and it doesn't need anyone or anything else to shine. Your inner light is a true reminder of the potential and possibilities in life. With focus, you can guide that light to expand and grow brighter and stronger, no matter what is happening in your life. Learn how bright you can shine in different situations and around different people. Allow your light to shine so bright it causes a ripple effect on those around you.

Condition yourself to always look within for not only the strength to go on when you are feeling down but for the strength to go further. In times of stress and strife, you must use your inner light to go further than you've ever gone. Don't let this breakup, or any other moment that comes your way break you, push! Push towards your happiness. Push towards your goals, push towards your dreams, and watch as everything you have ever desired begins to unfold in your life. The more we focus and run in the direction of our happiness, and our dreams, the more amazing things begin to unfold.

Realize today that you are the light, and you alone are any and everything you will ever need.

You are the light, and it is that light within you that you should always seek.

THE 28-DAY PROMISE

Congratulations - I am proud of you for making the decision to heal from heartbreak and stepping forward toward a better, happier you. I want you to think about the last chapter of this book and start to focus on your inner light. Make a promise to yourself that you will begin to tend to that familiar light inside. In times of adversity, when you are struggling to find your way through, look within. Cultivate that inner sunshine, by remembering all of the things we discussed throughout this book.

I PROMISE TO...

always light my own path! It is my birthright to be brilliant and to shine my light for all to see. I will use my light to guide me. When the days are dark and times get tough, I will always look for that light.

Monique T. Hicks

Author | Speaker

THANK YOU

Thank you for taking this journey with me. Writing this book has aided in my own healing, and some days I felt as if this book wrote itself. Someone once wrote that "when the Heroine returns from her journey with all she has learned, she brings that wisdom back to share with the world. And the women, men, and children of the world are transformed by her journey." I hope that you have been transformed.

I would love to stay in touch. Feel free to reach out to me on social media, and join my Facebook group 28 Days Under the Sun.

Please also help me get the word out about this book by leaving a review wherever you purchased this book. A good review will help this book reach the others who need it most.

SPECIAL OFFER

Stay tuned for special offers

Bibliography

Kessler, David. "Five Stages of Grief by Elisabeth Kubler Ross & David Kessler."
  Retrieved from Grief.com, grief.com/the-five-stages-of-grief/.

Depression (Major Depressive Disorder). 3 Feb. 2018,
  Retrieved from www.mayoclinic.org/diseases-conditions/depression/symptoms-causes/syc-20356007.

Healthy ways to deal with sadness - Gundersen Health System.
  Retrieved from https://www.gundersenhealth.org/health-wellness/live-n_happy/healthy-ways-to-deal-with-sadness/

Chadha, Raman. "The Junto Emotion Wheel: Why and How We Use It." The Junto Institute, The Junto Institute, 6
  June 2020,
  Retrieved from www.thejuntoinstitute.com/blog/the-junto-emotion-wheel-why-and-how-we-use-it.

Levin, Kendra. The Hero Is You: Sharpen Your Focus, Conquer Your Demons, and Become the Writer You Were
  Born to Be. Red Wheel/Weiser, LLC, 2016.

28 DAYS UNDER THE SUN